Standard Grade | General

French

Leckie×Leckie

First exam published in 2004.
Published by Leckie & Leckie Ltd, 3rd Floor, 4 Queen Street, Edinburgh EH2 1JE
tel: 0131 220 6831 fax: 0131 225 9987 enquiries@leckieandleckie.co.uk www.leckieandleckie.co.uk

ISBN 978-1-84372-630-2

A CIP Catalogue record for this book is available from the British Library.

Leckie & Leckie is a division of Huveaux plc.

Leckie & Leckie is grateful to the copyright holders, as credited at the back of the book, for permission to use their material.
Every effort has been made to trace the copyright holders and to obtain their permission for the use of copyright material.
Leckie & Leckie will gladly receive information enabling them to rectify any error or omission in subsequent editions.

[BLANK PAGE]

FOR OFFICIAL USE

G

Total

1000/402

NATIONAL
QUALIFICATIONS
2004

TUESDAY, 11 MAY
10.05 AM – 10.50 AM

FRENCH
STANDARD GRADE
General Level
Reading

Fill in these boxes and read what is printed below.

Full name of centre

Town

Forename(s)

Surname

Date of birth
Day   Month   Year

Scottish candidate number

Number of seat

When you are told to do so, open your paper and write your answers **in English** in the spaces provided.

You may use a French dictionary.

Before leaving the examination room you must give this book to the invigilator. If you do not, you may lose all the marks for this paper.

SCOTTISH
QUALIFICATIONS
AUTHORITY

THB 1000/402 6/45020

©

Marks

You are reading a French magazine.

1. Some primary school pupils give their opinions about school.

Que penses-tu de l'école?

Moi, j'aime aller à l'école pour les copains. La maîtresse est gentille, mais ce que je préfère vraiment, c'est la récréation!

Guillaume, 8 ans

J'aime ma maîtresse. Elle explique très bien et j'apprends beaucoup de choses avec elle. J'aime bien l'école, mais mon Papa et ma Maman me manquent.

Jacqueline, 9 ans

A l'école, je préfère le calcul et l'histoire. Mais, parfois, c'est fatigant aussi. J'aimerais avoir des consoles et des jeux-vidéo.

Paulette, 10 ans

Je n'aime pas l'école parce que je n'aime pas travailler. C'est ennuyeux. Je préfère rester chez moi, jouer avec mon chien.

Jean-Luc, 8 ans

Which of the pupils said the following?   3

Sometimes school is tiring.   _____

What I really like is the morning break.   _____

I'd rather stay at home.   _____

Marks

2. On the letters page of the magazine, you see this letter from a girl.

Je l'aime, comment lui dire?

Salut! Je veux bien inviter un garçon de ma classe
à sortir avec moi. Mais je suis très timide, et j'ai
peur de lui parler.
Je l'aime tellement. Aide-moi! Que dois-je faire?

Adrienne

(*a*) What does Adrienne want to do?   1

_____

_____

(*b*) Why does she find this difficult?
Mention any **one** thing.   1

_____

3. Then you read the advice given to the girl.

Conseil

Chère Adrienne!

Il y a beaucoup de filles qui sont comme toi. A ton
âge, c'est normal. Tu peux commencer en lui parlant
des choses que vous avez en commun, comme les
devoirs, les jeux-vidéo que tu préfères etc.

Complete the sentences.   2

She is told that many girls _____.

She should talk to him about _____

_____.

[Turn over

4. On another page of the magazine, you read some rules you should stick to when babysitting.

La Loi du Babysitter

Quand on garde des enfants, il ne faut jamais..........

- ......laisser un enfant seul

- ......utiliser le téléphone de la famille pour ses appels personnels

- ......inviter son petit copain

- ......fumer devant les enfants.

Complete the sentences.

You must never:

leave a child _____.

use _____.

invite _____.

smoke _____.

4

5. There is an article in the magazine about Harry Potter.

La Naissance de Harry Potter

Joanne Kathleen Rowling est née en Angleterre en 1967. Sa mère travaillait dans une bibliothèque, donc la petite Joanne lisait beaucoup.

Un jour, elle voyage en chemin de fer entre Manchester et Londres quand l'idée lui vient d'écrire l'histoire d'un petit sorcier nommé Harry.

Plus tard, en travaillant au Portugal, elle écrit trois chapitres du premier livre "Harry Potter".

Elle revient vivre à Edimbourg, en Ecosse, où elle termine son livre. Elle l'envoie à des agents littéraires, mais ils le refusent. Après un an, elle trouve un éditeur qui veut bien le publier.

Mais le succès n'est pas instantané; ce n'est qu'avec la parution du troisième livre que les aventures de Harry deviennent célèbres partout dans le monde et que J. K. Rowling fait sa fortune.

(a) Why did J. K. Rowling read a lot when she was a child? **1**

_____

(b) Where did she first have the idea of writing about Harry? **1**

_____

(c) What did she do in Portugal? **1**

_____

(d) Why did it take so long for the book to appear?
Give any **one** reason. **1**

_____

(e) What happened when the third book appeared?
Mention **two** things. **2**

_____

_____

[Turn over

DO NOT
WRITE IN
THIS
MARGIN

Marks

6. You read about a new use for the Internet.

L'Internet à l'Hôpital

Tous les jours, il y a 150 000 enfants à l'hôpital en France. Bien sûr, ils sont malades, mais souvent, ils souffrent aussi de l'isolement.

Maintenant, plusieurs hôpitaux ont installé des ordinateurs et des liaisons Internet. Comme ça, les enfants restent en contact avec leur école et peuvent communiquer avec leurs copains.

En général, les médecins sont pour cette idée, car ça permet aux enfants de guérir plus vite.

(*a*) When children are ill in hospital, what other problem do they often have?

1

(*b*) How does having access to the Internet help the children?

2

(*c*) Why are doctors in favour of this use of the Internet?

1

DO NOT
WRITE IN
THIS
MARGIN

Marks

7. One day, your pen pal's sister shows you a letter she has written to a hotel in England.

Fabienne GARNIER,
16, rue des Rosiers,
45360 MONTCLAIR,
France

Royal Hotel,
LEICESTER
Angleterre

Monsieur,

J'ai lu sur votre site web que vous cherchez un(e) jeune Français(e) pour travailler dans votre hôtel pendant les mois de juillet et d'août.

J'ai 19 ans et, pendant mes vacances scolaires, j'ai déjà travaillé dans un petit hôtel ici à Montclair. Dans ce travail, j'ai souvent parlé avec des touristes britanniques.

Je voudrais bien passer quelques mois en Grande-Bretagne pour perfectionner mon anglais et me renseigner sur les différences entre les hôtels français et les hôtels britanniques.

Je vous prie d'agréer, Monsieur, mes sincères salutations.

Fabienne Garnier

(*a*) What has Fabienne done previously during her school holidays?   1

_____

(*b*) How has this prepared her for working in Great Britain?   1

_____

(*c*) Why does she want to spend time in Great Britain?   2

_____

_____

_____

[Turn over

Marks

8. In a newspaper, you read this article about a young driver.

Attention! Petite au volant!

Dans la ville de Sydney, en Australie, une petite fille de huit ans a décidé de conduire la voiture de sa mère.

La voiture était dans le parking d'un supermarché où sa mère faisait des courses.

La petite voulait rentrer à la maison toute seule dans la voiture.

Heureusement, après quelques centaines de mètres, un policier a réussi à arrêter la voiture.

Tick (✓) **True** or **False** for each sentence.

4

	True	False
An eight-year-old girl was driving a car.		
Her mother had given her the keys.		
Her mother was shopping at the time.		
The girl drove into a police car.		

9. On another page, you read an unusual story about a postcard.

> **E-MAIL – QUELQUES SECONDES**
>
> **POSTE – SOIXANTE-TREIZE ANS**
>
> Grâce à l'Internet, un message électronique met quelques secondes à parcourir la planète.
>
> Ce n'est pas le cas d'une certaine carte postale. Envoyée il y a soixante-treize ans, elle est arrivée à sa destination cette année au mois de février.
>
> Malheureusement, la destinataire est morte. Mais sa fille, qui habite toujours la même adresse, a reçu la carte.

Complete the sentences.

An electronic message takes only a few seconds to _____

_____.

The postcard was sent _____.

The person it was sent to has died, but her daughter received the card

because _____.

3

Total (32)

[END OF QUESTION PAPER]

[BLANK PAGE]

G

1000/407

NATIONAL QUALIFICATIONS 2004	TUESDAY, 11 MAY 1.45 PM – 2.10 PM (APPROX)	FRENCH STANDARD GRADE General Level Listening Transcript

This paper must not be seen by any candidate.

The material overleaf is provided for use in an emergency only (eg the recording or equipment proving faulty) or where permission has been given in advance by SQA for the material to be read to candidates with special needs. The material must be read exactly as printed.

SCOTTISH
QUALIFICATIONS
AUTHORITY

©

Transcript—General Level

Instructions to reader(s):

For each item, read the English **once**, then read the French **three times**, with an interval of 5 seconds between the readings. On completion of the third reading, pause for the length of time indicated in brackets after each item, to allow the candidates to write their answers.

Where special arrangements have been agreed in advance to allow the reading of the material, those sections marked **(f)** should be read by a female speaker and those marked **(m)** by a male: those sections marked **(t)** should be read by the teacher.

(t) You are spending two weeks at the home of your French pen pal, Julie.

(m) or (f) **Tu passes des vacances chez ta correspondante française, Julie.**

(t) Question number one.

When you arrive, Julie's father speaks to you.

What does he ask you? Tick **three** boxes.

(m) **Tu es fatigué après ton voyage? Tu vas passer combien de temps ici? Tu as déjà visité la France?**

(30 seconds)

(t) Question number two.

Julie tells you about the plans for tomorrow.

What will you be doing? Complete the sentences.

(f) **Demain, on va passer la journée en ville. Tu sais, le samedi matin, il y a un marché sur la place. L'après-midi, on va au centre sportif voir mes copains.**

(30 seconds)

(t) Question number three.

Julie talks about someone she wants you to meet during your stay.

Who is this person? What is he organising?

(f) **Je dois te présenter à mon professeur d'anglais. Il organise un voyage scolaire pour nous. On va visiter le sud de l'Angleterre.**

(30 seconds)

(t) Question number four.

Julie's dad tells you he works for a shop which sells electrical goods.

What exactly does he do? Tick **one** box.

(m) **Je ne travaille pas dans le magasin. Quand un client achète une nouvelle machine à laver ou un nouveau frigo, moi, je vais chez le client pour installer la machine.**

(30 seconds)

(t) Question number five.

He tells you more about his job.

Why does he like it? Mention **two** things.

(m)　　　**C'est bien parce qu'on rencontre beaucoup de gens, et ce que j'aime le plus, c'est que je travaille seul.**

(30 seconds)

(t) Question number six.

Julie says you will be going to a football match at the weekend.

Who is playing?

(f)　　　**Ça va être passionnant. C'est un match entre deux équipes de première division.**

(30 seconds)

(t) Question number seven.

Julie tells you about the football stadium.

Tick **True** or **False** for each sentence.

(f)　　　**C'est un stade très moderne, près de la ville. Il y a des places pour trente mille spectateurs et un parking énorme derrière le stade.**

(30 seconds)

(t) Question number eight.

She tells you about the tickets for the match.

When did her dad buy them? How much did they cost?

(f)　　　**En France, les matchs de foot coûtent cher. Mon père a acheté les billets la semaine dernière. Il a payé quarante euros le billet.**

(30 seconds)

(t) Question number nine.

Julie then tells you what you will be doing in the second week of your stay.

Complete the sentences.

(f)　　　**On va passer une semaine chez ma tante. Elle habite à la montagne, près de la frontière espagnole.**

(30 seconds)

[Turn over for Questions 10 to 12 on *Page four*

(t) Question number ten.

Julie talks about the journey there.

How long will it take? Why will you travel by car?

(f)   **Pour y aller, ça fait cinq heures et demie de route. Mais la voiture est pratique parce que nous avons beaucoup de bagages.**

(30 seconds)

(t) Question number eleven.

You will have several stops during your journey.

Why? Give any **one** reason.

(f)   **On va s'arrêter plusieurs fois pendant le voyage. Ma petite soeur n'aime pas tellement les voyages en voiture. Souvent, elle se sent malade.**

(30 seconds)

(t) Question number twelve.

Julie talks about the things you can do while you are there.

What can you do there? Mention any **three** things.

(f)   **A la montagne, on peut faire de l'escalade, bien sûr. Mais on peut aussi faire des promenades à pied, et à cheval. Il y a même un petit lac où on peut faire de la voile.**

(30 seconds)

(t) End of test.

Now look over your answers.

[END OF TRANSCRIPT]

FOR OFFICIAL USE

G

Total Mark

1000/406

NATIONAL
QUALIFICATIONS
2004

TUESDAY, 11 MAY
1.45 PM – 2.10 PM
(APPROX)

FRENCH
STANDARD GRADE
General Level
Listening

Fill in these boxes and read what is printed below.

Full name of centre

Town

Forename(s)

Surname

Date of birth
 Day Month Year   Scottish candidate number   Number of seat

When you are told to do so, open your paper.

You will hear a number of short items in French. You will hear each item three times, then you will have time to write your answer.

Write your answers, **in English**, in this book, in the appropriate spaces.

You may take notes as you are listening to the French, but only in this paper.

You may **not** use a French dictionary.

You are not allowed to leave the examination room until the end of the test.

Before leaving the examination room you must give this book to the invigilator. If you do not, you may lose all the marks for this paper.

SCOTTISH
QUALIFICATIONS
AUTHORITY

THB 1000/406 6/45020

Marks

You are spending two weeks at the home of your French pen pal, Julie.

Tu passes des vacances chez ta correspondante française, Julie.

1. When you arrive, Julie's father speaks to you. What does he ask you?
    Tick (✓) **three** boxes.

    3

Are you tired after your journey?	
How long are you staying?	
How long was your journey?	
How do you like France?	
Have you been to France before?	
Are you hungry?	

    *   *   *   *   *

2. Julie tells you about the plans for tomorrow. What will you be doing?
    Complete the sentences.

    3

    You will be spending the day _____.

    In the morning there is a _____.

    In the afternoon, you will go to the sports centre to _____

    _____.

    *   *   *   *   *

3. Julie talks about someone she wants you to meet during your stay.

    (*a*) Who is this person?

    1

    _____

    (*b*) What is he organising?

    1

    _____

    *   *   *   *   *

Marks

4. Julie's dad tells you he works for a shop which sells electrical goods. What exactly does he do? Tick (✓) **one** box.

He sells washing machines and fridges to customers.	
He installs washing machines and fridges in customers' homes.	
He repairs washing machines and fridges for customers.	

1

*   *   *   *   *

5. He tells you more about his job. Why does he like it? Mention **two** things.

_____

_____

2

*   *   *   *   *

6. Julie says you will be going to a football match at the weekend. Who is playing?

_____

1

*   *   *   *   *

7. Julie tells you about the football stadium. Tick (✓) **True** or **False** for each sentence.

	True	False
The stadium is in the town centre.		
It holds 50,000 spectators.		
There is a large car park behind the stadium.		

3

*   *   *   *   *

[Turn over for Questions 8 to 12 on _Page four_

Marks

8. She tells you about the tickets for the match.

    (*a*) When did her dad buy them?

        _____

1

    (*b*) How much did they cost?

        _____

1

*   *   *   *   *

9. Julie then tells you what you will be doing in the second week of your stay. Complete the sentences.

You will spend a week at _____

in the _____ , near the _____ border.

3

*   *   *   *   *

10. Julie talks about the journey there.

    (*a*) How long will it take?

        _____

1

    (*b*) Why will you travel by car?

        _____

1

*   *   *   *   *

11. You will have several stops during your journey. Why? Give any **one** reason.

_____

1

*   *   *   *   *

12. Julie talks about the things you can do while you are there. What can you do there? Mention any **three** things.

_____

_____

_____

3

*   *   *   *   *

Total (26)

[*END OF QUESTION PAPER*]

[BLANK PAGE]

FOR OFFICIAL USE

G

Total

1000/402

NATIONAL
QUALIFICATIONS
2005

TUESDAY, 10 MAY
10.05 AM – 10.50 AM

**FRENCH
STANDARD GRADE**
General Level
Reading

Fill in these boxes and read what is printed below.

Full name of centre

Town

Forename(s)

Surname

Date of birth
Day Month Year   Scottish candidate number   Number of seat

When you are told to do so, open your paper and write your answers **in English** in the spaces provided.

You may use a French dictionary.

Before leaving the examination room you must give this book to the invigilator. If you do not, you may lose all the marks for this paper.

SCOTTISH
QUALIFICATIONS
AUTHORITY

©

Marks

You are reading a French magazine.

1. You find an article about Catherine Zeta-Jones.

Divine Catherine

Catherine Zeta-Jones avait six ans quand un directeur de théâtre l'a remarquée dans un spectacle. Il lui a proposé le rôle d' "Annie" dans la comédie musicale. Elle s'est installée ensuite à Londres à l'âge de quinze ans comme *doublure de l'actrice principale dans "42ème Rue".

*doublure – stand-in.

(*a*)   Catherine Zeta-Jones got her first big break at the age of six.

How did it happen? Mention **two** things.

2

_____

_____

_____

(*b*)   What was her rôle in "42nd Street"?

1

_____

Page two

Marks

2. The article goes on.

Les passions de Catherine

Catherine a une passion pour la musique et la lecture. "Mon père avait l'habitude de me réveiller avec les chansons d'Elvis Presley et de Van Morrison." Maintenant elle avoue avoir une passion pour les chansons de Céline Dion.

Et son roman préféré? C'est toujours "The Great Gatsby". "Je l'ai lu pour la première fois à treize ans et je le relis régulièrement."

(a) She has a great love of music.

How does she explain this?

1

(b) What does she say about her favourite book "The Great Gatsby"?

Mention any **one** thing.

1

[Turn over

Marks

3. You read about a new idea for postage stamps in Finland.

> ## Timbres personnalisés!
>
> En Finlande, tu pourras bientôt timbrer une lettre avec ta propre photo.
>
> La Poste finlandaise propose de fabriquer des timbres avec les visages de citoyens individuels à la place des personnages célèbres.
>
> Mais ce timbre coûtera un peu plus cher qu'un timbre normal.

Complete the sentences.

3

In Finland, people will be able to get a stamp with _____

_____.

The Post Office will put this on instead of pictures of _____

_____.

The stamp will _____

_____.

Marks

4. You read an article about Grandmothers' Day in France.

"Bonne Fête, Mamie!"

Le premier dimanche de mars, les grand-mères sont à l'honneur. Les mamies sont sept millions en France et plus de la moitié d'entre elles voient leurs petits-enfants une fois par semaine. Les grand-mères sont de plus en plus jeunes: quarante-huit pour cent d'entre elles ont moins de soixante-cinq ans.

(a) When is Grandmothers' Day celebrated in France?

1

_____

(b) According to the article how often do most grandmothers see their grandchildren?

1

_____

(c) What are we told about 48% of grandmothers?

1

_____

[Turn over

Marks

5. The article talks about this year's "Super Gran".

LA SUPER MAMIE!

Depuis sept ans, un concours a lieu chaque année pour récompenser la Super Mamie: une grand-mère dynamique et pleine de talents. Cette année la Super Mamie est Juliette Fourvel, une grand-mère de soixante-trois ans, qui compose des chansons, écrit des poésies, pratique le vélo, et fait du ski nautique!

Juliette Fourvel was the latest grandmother to win the title "Super Mamie". What activities does she take part in?

Mention any **two** things.

2

_____

_____

6. There is an article about a chef.

Chef cuisinier et patron de restaurant!
Louis Picaud raconte sa journée!

Alors, chaque matin je vais choisir mes poissons et ma viande au marché. Quand je reviens, je prépare la carte du jour et on commence à travailler dans la cuisine. Il y a deux services, à midi et à dix-neuf heures. Le soir, je fais les comptes avec ma femme.

J'ai commencé à quatorze ans. J'aidais mon père dans son restaurant. Puis, comme apprenti, j'ai travaillé dans les grands restaurants de plusieurs villes. J'ai appris à préparer les spécialités de toutes les régions.

Ensuite, j'ai ouvert mon propre restaurant, et maintenant j'ai trois jeunes apprentis qui travaillent chez moi.

Complete the sentences.

In the mornings, Louis goes to the market to buy _____.

Then he prepares the day's _____.

In the evening his wife helps him with _____.

As an apprentice chef he worked in restaurants in _____.

Now he has _____.

5

[Turn over

DO NOT
WRITE IN
THIS
MARGIN

Marks

7. On the letters page, a girl has written in with a problem.

Mon Problème

Je mange trop de bonbons. Je sais que ce n'est pas bon pour la santé, mais quand on me propose un bonbon, je ne peux pas refuser. Que dois-je faire?

Marie, 14 ans

(*a*) What is Marie's problem?

1

_____

(*b*) How does this happen?

1

_____

Marks

8. You read the magazine's answer to Marie's problem.

> ### *Réponse*
>
> Tu n'es pas la seule à ne pas résister aux bonbons, mais la solution est de prendre des repas équilibrés.
>
> Tu as besoin de quatre repas par jour. Les plus importants sont le petit déjeuner et le repas de midi. Si tu manges bien à ces deux repas, tu n'auras pas faim dans la journée. Il te faut des produits laitiers, de la viande, des légumes et des fruits.
>
> **Sophie**

(a) How does Sophie suggest Marie can change her bad habit?

1

_____

(b) What does Sophie say about breakfast and lunch?

1

_____

(c) Apart from meat and fruit, what else does Marie need to eat at these meals?

Mention **two** things.

2

_____

_____

[Turn over

Mark

9. There is a story about some mysterious thefts.

Qui vole les ordinateurs?

Mercredi, on a volé deux ordinateurs à une grande entreprise à Vannes. C'est la cinquième fois depuis novembre. Au total, quatorze appareils ont disparu.

Le chef de l'entreprise est perplexe.
"Sans doute, c'est quelqu'un qui connaît notre entreprise", dit-il. "Les nouveaux appareils sont sur place pendant deux ou trois jours seulement, et les cambrioleurs arrivent."

Comme les alarmes n'ont pas dissuadé les cambrioleurs, les gendarmes utilisent maintenant un hélicoptère pour surveiller la zone la nuit.

Tick (✓) the **three** correct sentences.

3

The stolen items were computers.	
It's the third time this has happened.	
The boss thinks it's someone who knows the company.	
The thefts take place every two or three days.	
Alarms have been effective in stopping the thefts.	
The police are using a helicopter to patrol the area at night.	

Marks

10. You read about the French sprinter, Muriel Hurtis.

Muriel Hurtis
- athlète extraordinaire!

Muriel Hurtis est née le 25 mars, 1979. Elle grandit en Seine-Saint-Denis dans la région parisienne. Au collège, elle découvre l'athlétisme par hasard. Un jour, elle va au stade avec une copine et le prof de sport la voit.

En 1998, Muriel obtient son baccalauréat en sciences. Cette année-là, elle gagne une médaille d'or sur 200 mètres aux Championnats du Monde Juniors à Annecy – son premier succès public.

Tick (✓) **True** or **False** for each sentence.

3

	True	**False**
Muriel got into athletics by chance.		
Her PE teacher took her to the stadium one day.		
In 1998, she won a gold medal for the 200 metres.		

[Turn over for Question 11 on *Page twelve*

Marks

11. The article continues.

"Courir, c'est ma passion!"

Muriel est membre de l'équipe Française 4 x 100 mètres, mais elle préfère toujours les 200 mètres individuels, où elle est presque invincible.

"Courir, c'est ma passion, mais l'athlétisme ne va pas durer pour toujours. Quand ma vie d'athlète sera finie, il sera nécessaire de trouver un métier. Voilà pourquoi j'ai commencé des études de comptabilité."

Tick (✓) **True** or **False** for each sentence.   2

	True	False
Muriel prefers the 200 metres because she is almost unbeatable at that distance.		
When her running is over, Muriel hopes to become an athletics coach.		

Total (32)

[END OF QUESTION PAPER]

G

1000/407

NATIONAL QUALIFICATIONS 2005	TUESDAY, 10 MAY 1.45 PM – 2.10 PM (APPROX)	**FRENCH STANDARD GRADE** General Level Listening Transcript

This paper must not be seen by any candidate.

The material overleaf is provided for use in an emergency only (eg the recording or equipment proving faulty) or where permission has been given in advance by SQA for the material to be read to candidates with special needs. The material must be read exactly as printed.

SCOTTISH
QUALIFICATIONS
AUTHORITY

Transcript—General Level

Instructions to reader(s):

For each item, read the English **once**, then read the French **three times**, with an interval of 5 seconds between the readings. On completion of the third reading, pause for the length of time indicated in brackets after each item, to allow the candidates to write their answers.

Where special arrangements have been agreed in advance to allow the reading of the material, those sections marked **(f)** should be read by a female speaker and those marked **(m)** by a male: those sections marked **(t)** should be read by the teacher.

(t) You are staying with your French penpal, Julie, in the Loire Valley.

(m) or (f) **Tu loges chez ta correspondante française, Julie, dans la vallée de la Loire.**

(30 seconds)

(t) Question number one.

You have just arrived. What does Julie ask you?

(f) **Tu veux quelque chose à manger?**

(30 seconds)

(t) Question number two.

She tells you about the village she lives in. What does she say about it?

Tick **two** boxes.

(f) **Pont-Saint-Martin c'est un petit village tout près de Nantes. Dans le village il y a une petite église, la mairie et plusieurs magasins.**

(30 seconds)

(t) Question number three.

She tells you about events which are happening the next day. What are they?

Tick the **two** correct boxes.

(f) **Demain après-midi il y aura un concours de natation et le soir il y aura un festival de danse.**

(30 seconds)

(t) Question number four.

She introduces you to her sister, Nathalie. What does Nathalie tell you?

Complete the sentences.

(f) **Il y a cinq ans je travaillais comme assistante de français en Ecosse. Je partageais un appartement avec une assistante italienne. Au collège je parlais de la vie en France à mes élèves et je les aidais à parler français.**

(30 seconds)

(t) Question number five.

Nathalie talks about her time in Scotland and the friends she made. What does she say? Mention any **three** things.

(f) Je garde un excellent souvenir de cette année qui a passé très vite. Aujourd'hui je suis toujours en contact avec trois assistants, un Allemand, un Espagnol et une Italienne. Tous les ans, on se voit pendant les vacances.

(30 seconds)

(t) Question number six.

She goes on to tell you about her job. What does she say about her job with France Télécom?

Mention any **two** things.

(f) Je travaille pour France Télécom depuis deux ans. Quand j'ai commencé le travail était difficile. Mais maintenant j'ai de bons collègues et tout le monde s'entend bien.

(30 seconds)

(t) Question number seven.

Julie's father comes home and starts talking to you. What does he tell you?

Complete the sentences.

(m) Moi, j'adore l'Ecosse. J'ai visité l'Ecosse pour la première fois en dix-neuf cent quatre-vingt-dix. On a fait un échange de maisons avec une famille écossaise car nous n'avions pas beaucoup d'argent. Je retourne en Ecosse tous les deux ans pour les matchs de rugby et aussi pour les vacances.

(30 seconds)

(t) Question number eight.

He goes on to talk about his interest in whisky. What does he say? Mention any **two** things.

(m) Quand je suis en Ecosse, j'aime bien visiter des distilleries. J'en ai déjà visité quatre dans les Highlands. J'ai une grande collection de whisky et parfois j'offre une bouteille de whisky à des amis.

(30 seconds)

(t) Question number nine.

He tells you about the wine industry in the area. What does he say about the Loire Valley? Mention **one** thing. What does he say about his wine collection? Mention any **one** thing.

(m) Ici on cultive la vigne. La vallée de la Loire est très célèbre pour le vin. Quant à moi, j'ai plus de cent bouteilles de vin dans la cave. J'ai même une bouteille qui date de dix-neuf cent cinquante-sept.

(30 seconds)

[Turn over for Questions 10 to 12 on *Page four*

(t) **Question number ten.**

He suggests that you visit the castle of Chambord. Are the statements below **True** or **False**?

Tick the correct boxes.

(m) **Il faut visiter le château de Chambord qui est situé dans une grande forêt. C'est le plus grand château de la région et on dit qu'il y a une cheminée pour chaque jour de l'année.**

(30 seconds)

(t) **Question number eleven.**

Julie doesn't think it's a good idea. Why not? Mention **two** things.

(f) **Mais tu sais, Papa, qu'il y a toujours beaucoup de touristes au château et ça coûte assez cher.**

(30 seconds)

(t) **Question number twelve.**

Before Julie's dad goes out, he says something to you. What does he say?

(m) **Amuse-toi bien pendant ton séjour en France!**

(30 seconds)

(t) **End of test.**

Now look over your answers.

[END OF TRANSCRIPT]

FOR OFFICIAL USE

G

Total Mark

1000/406

NATIONAL QUALIFICATIONS 2005

TUESDAY, 10 MAY 1.45 PM – 2.10 PM (APPROX)

FRENCH STANDARD GRADE General Level Listening

Fill in these boxes and read what is printed below.

Full name of centre

Town

Forename(s)

Surname

Date of birth
Day Month Year

Scottish candidate number

Number of seat

When you are told to do so, open your paper.

You will hear a number of short items in French. You will hear each item three times, then you will have time to write your answer.

Write your answers, **in English**, in this book, in the appropriate spaces.

You may take notes as you are listening to the French, but only in this paper.

You may **not** use a French dictionary.

You are not allowed to leave the examination room until the end of the test.

Before leaving the examination room you must give this book to the invigilator. If you do not, you may lose all the marks for this paper.

SCOTTISH QUALIFICATIONS AUTHORITY

Marks

You are staying with your French penpal, Julie, in the Loire Valley.

Tu loges chez ta correspondante française, Julie, dans la vallée de la Loire.

1. You have just arrived. What does Julie ask you?

_____

1

*   *   *   *   *

2. She tells you about the village she lives in. What does she say about it? Tick
(✓) **two** boxes.

2

It's quite far from Nantes.	
It has a small church.	
There is a town hall.	
There are no shops.	

*   *   *   *   *

3. She tells you about events which are happening the next day. What are they?
Tick (✓) the **two** correct boxes.

2

*   *   *   *   *

Marks

4. She introduces you to her sister, Nathalie. What does Nathalie tell you? Complete the sentences.

    _____ years ago, she worked as a French assistant in Scotland.

She _____ with an Italian assistant. She spoke to

the pupils about _____ in France and helped them to speak French.

3

*   *   *   *   *

5. Nathalie talks about her time in Scotland and the friends she made. What does she say? Mention any **three** things.

_____

_____

_____

3

*   *   *   *   *

6. She goes on to tell you about her job. What does she say about her job with France Télécom? Mention any **two** things.

_____

_____

2

*   *   *   *   *

7. Julie's father comes home and starts talking to you. What does he tell you? Complete the sentences.

In 1990 he came to Scotland _____.

They did a house exchange because _____

_____.

He comes back to Scotland _____

for rugby matches and for holidays.

3

*   *   *   *   *

[Turn over for Questions 8 to 12 on *Page four*

Marks

8. He goes on to talk about his interest in whisky. What does he say? Mention any **two** things.

2

_____

_____

*   *   *   *   *

9. He tells you about the wine industry in the area.

(*a*)   What does he say about the Loire Valley? Mention **one** thing.

1

_____

(*b*)   What does he say about his wine collection? Mention any **one** thing.

1

_____

*   *   *   *   *

10. He suggests that you visit the castle of Chambord. Are the statements below **True** or **False**? Tick (✓) the correct boxes.

3

	True	False
It's situated in a park.		
It's the largest castle in the area.		
There is a chimney for every day of the year.		

*   *   *   *   *

11. Julie doesn't think it's a good idea. Why not? Mention **two** things.

2

_____

_____

*   *   *   *   *

12. Before Julie's dad goes out, he says something to you. What does he say?

1

_____

*   *   *   *   *

Total (26)

[END OF QUESTION PAPER]

[BLANK PAGE]

FOR OFFICIAL USE

G

Total ☐

1000/402

NATIONAL
QUALIFICATIONS
2006

TUESDAY, 9 MAY
10.05 AM – 10.50 AM

**FRENCH
STANDARD GRADE**
General Level
Reading

Fill in these boxes and read what is printed below.

Full name of centre

Town

Forename(s)

Surname

Date of birth
Day Month Year   Scottish candidate number   Number of seat

When you are told to do so, open your paper and write your answers **in English** in the spaces provided.

You may use a French dictionary.

Before leaving the examination room you must give this book to the invigilator. If you do not, you may lose all the marks for this paper.

SCOTTISH
QUALIFICATIONS
AUTHORITY

©

Marks

You are staying with your pen-pal in France.

You are reading a French magazine.

1. Jacqueline has written to the magazine about a problem she has with her little brother.

Mon petit frère m'embête!

Salut!

Mon petit frère m'énerve! Il veut toujours savoir où je vais et il veut m'accompagner tout le temps. Mais à l'âge de neuf ans, il est trop jeune pour sortir avec moi. Que faire?

Jacqueline, 13 ans

(a) How does Jacqueline's brother annoy her? Mention **two** things.

2

_____

_____

(b) Why will Jacqueline not do what he wants? Mention any **one** thing.

1

_____

Page two

Marks

2. There is an article in the magazine about bringing a beach to Paris.

Une Plage à Paris

Pendant les quatre semaines du mois d'août, les Parisiens ont une plage chez eux.

Le maire de Paris a fait apporter des tonnes de sable sur les bords de la rivière Seine. On a apporté aussi des chaises, des parasols et des palmiers.

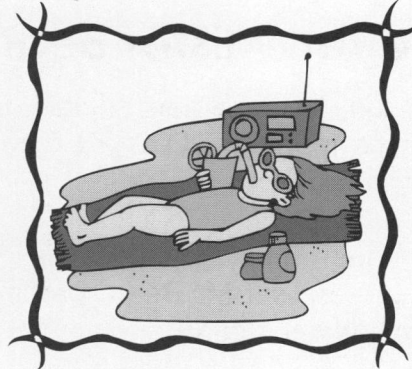

On ne peut pas nager, car l'eau est trop polluée, mais il y a des jets d'eau pour rafraîchir le public. Le soir, on propose des spectacles, et même des dîners!

Tick (✓) the **three** correct sentences.

3

There will be a beach in Paris for two weeks in August.	
Tons of sand have been brought to the river Seine.	
There are also seats, parasols and palm trees.	
People will be able to swim in the river.	
Jets of water will be used to clean the sand.	
At night there will be shows and dinners.	

[Turn over

Marks

3. In the magazine there is an article about the English comedian, Rowan Atkinson.

Blackadder. Mister Bean . . . et quoi encore?

Rowan Atkinson, le comédien anglais, visite la France en ce moment. D'abord il nous a parlé de sa carrière.

"J'ai aimé tous mes rôles, mais mon personnage préféré est Mr Bean, parce qu'il fait de la comédie sans parler."

Puis il a parlé de "Johnny English", un film comique qui raconte les aventures d'un agent secret anglais. Johnny English voudrait être comme James Bond, mais il trouve des désastres partout!

"Dans 'Johnny English', j'ai adoré les courses en voiture. Vous savez, les voitures de sport, c'est ma passion!"

"Et Mr Bean? Il est 'en retraite' en ce moment. Mais il va revenir un jour, sans doute."

(*a*) Why does Rowan Atkinson prefer Mr Bean to his other roles? Mention **one** thing.

1

(*b*) What does the article say about Johnny English, the English secret agent? Mention any **one** thing.

1

(*c*) Why did he enjoy the car chases in "Johnny English" so much? Mention **one** thing.

1

(*d*) What does Rowan say finally about Mr Bean? Mention **two** things.

2

Marks

4. You read an article about a disaster on the Pacific island of Fiji.

Pluies Torrentielles au Fidji

Hier, près de 8 000 personnes ont été obligées de quitter leurs maisons et de partir dans la haute terre de l'île principale du Fidji. C'est la suite de dix jours de pluie ininterrompue.

Huit personnes sont mortes, onze autres ont disparu.

Le gouvernement du pays a promis de l'aide financière pour les habitants qui ont perdu leurs domiciles.

Complete the sentences.   **4**

About 8000 people had to _____.

The disaster was caused by ten days of _____.

Eleven people have _____.

The government will help people who _____

_____.

[Turn over

Marks

5. You read an article about smoking on trains in France.

Plus de cigarettes dans les TGV

A partir de décembre, tous les TGV (Trains à Grande Vitesse) seront complètement non-fumeurs.

*La SNCF applique des règles anti-tabacs plus strictes pour préserver la santé des voyageurs.

Un sondage récent indique que la plupart des gens préfèrent voyager dans les wagons non-fumeurs.

Bientôt, quand les trains s'arrêteront dans les gares, on verra beaucoup de gens descendre sur le quai pour fumer leur cigarette.

*La SNCF – French Railways

(*a*) What will happen to TGV trains in December? Mention **one** thing.

1

_____

(*b*) Why is the SNCF applying this rule? Mention **one** thing.

1

_____

(*c*) What does a recent survey indicate? Mention **one** thing.

1

_____

(*d*) What is likely to happen when trains stop at stations? Mention **one** thing.

1

_____

Marks

6. There is also a story about an unusual World Cup competition.

Parc du FUTUROSCOPE

Au Parc du Futuroscope à Poitiers, entre le 6 et 12 juillet, on peut voir la Coupe du Monde des jeux-vidéo. Près de quarante nationalités sont représentées. En tout, il y a plus de trois cents joueurs qui participent aux jeux.

Tous les matchs sont transmis sur écrans géants et il y a des commentaires pour le grand public. Les organisateurs attendent plus de 25 000 personnes pendant les sept jours du tournoi.

Tick (✓) the **three** correct sentences.

3

There is to be a World Cup for video games.	
Fourteen nationalities are represented.	
There are over three hundred games to be played.	
The matches are shown on giant screens.	
Members of the public give commentaries on the games.	
The organisers expect more than 25 000 people to attend over seven days.	

[Turn over

Marks

7. You read an article about travel.

Tu aimes voyager?

Selon un sondage, huit enfants sur dix sont déjà partis à l'étranger et environ 40% d'entre eux partent chaque année. Les destinations les plus populaires sont l'Europe, suivi des Etats-Unis et de l'Afrique.

En général les enfants ont envie de découvrir d'autres pays et de faire la connaissance d'autres personnes.

Complete the sentences.

(*a*) 8 children in 10 have _____ 1

_____.

(*b*) Europe, USA and Africa are _____ 1

_____.

(*c*) In general children like discovering other countries and _____ 1

_____.

Marks

8. You read an article about where people live.

Où j'habite

> La campagne ne me dit rien. Je suis né dans une grande ville et j'espère y passer toute ma vie.
>
> *Eric*

> J'habite en ville mais ça ne me plaît pas. Heureusement je peux passer les grandes vacances chez mes grands-parents qui habitent toujours à la campagne.
>
> *Jérôme*

> J'aimerais déménager à la campagne. L'air est pur, et il n'y a pas de pollution comme en ville.
>
> *Thierry*

> En ville on ne s'ennuie pas. Il y a toujours beaucoup à faire et à voir. Tout se trouve près de la maison – les magasins, les boîtes, les maisons des jeunes.
>
> *Amélie*

> J'ai toujours habité dans une ferme mais on est loin de tout – loin des copains, loin des magasins. En plus, on est toujours seul pendant les vacances.
>
> *Stéphanie*

Who made these statements? Put the correct name in each box.

3

I can spend holidays in the countryside.	
I would like to spend the rest of my life in a town.	
I am alone during the holidays.	

[Turn over

Marks

9. Your pen-pal shows you a letter he has received about the summer job he will have this year.

Camping du Pré Vert

Cher Monsieur,

Pendant les mois de juillet et d'août, vous allez travailler à la réception du camping.

Vous allez travailler 35 heures par semaine, c'est-à-dire sept heures par jour, cinq jours par semaine.

Vous allez . . .
- enregistrer les clients
- aider les clients à s'installer dans les caravanes et sur les emplacements
- accepter les réservations par téléphone
- distribuer les bouteilles de gaz aux clients.

Vous devez arriver sur place le 30 juin.

Amitiés,

Jacques Pinot, Directeur du Camping

(*a*) How will your pen-pal's working week of 35 hours be organised? Mention **two** things.

2

_____

_____

(*b*) What duties will he have? Mention any **two** things.

2

_____

_____

Total (32)

[END OF QUESTION PAPER]

G

1000/407

NATIONAL
QUALIFICATIONS
2006

TUESDAY, 9 MAY
1.45 PM – 2.10 PM
(APPROX)

FRENCH
STANDARD GRADE
General Level
Listening Transcript

This paper must not be seen by any candidate.

The material overleaf is provided for use in an emergency only (eg the recording or equipment proving faulty) or where permission has been given in advance by SQA for the material to be read to candidates with additional support needs. The material must be read exactly as printed.

SCOTTISH
QUALIFICATIONS
AUTHORITY

Transcript—General Level

Instructions to reader(s):

For each item, read the English **once**, then read the French **three times**, with an interval of 5 seconds between the readings. On completion of the third reading, pause for the length of time indicated in brackets after each item, to allow the candidates to write their answers.

Where special arrangements have been agreed in advance to allow the reading of the material, those sections marked **(f)** should be read by a female speaker and those marked **(m)** by a male: those sections marked **(t)** should be read by the teacher.

(t) You are spending your holidays with your family on a campsite in France.

(m) or (f) **Tu passes les vacances avec ta famille dans un camping en France.**

(t) Question number one.

When you arrive, you meet a French boy, Antoine. What does he ask you?

(m) **C'est ta première visite en France?**

(30 seconds)

(t) Question number two.

He introduces you to his family. His mother tells you about the campsite. What does she say?

Tick **three** boxes.

(f) **Le camping n'est pas très grand et c'est vraiment tranquille ici. Il y a beaucoup à faire pour les enfants, par exemple il y a une piscine en plein air et une salle de jeux.**

(30 seconds)

(t) Question number three.

She tells you about their journey to the campsite. What does she say?

Complete the sentences.

(f) **Nous habitons à trois cents kilomètres du camping. Normalement, il nous faut quatre heures pour le voyage mais il y avait un accident sur l'autoroute, donc le voyage a duré six heures.**

(30 seconds)

(t) Question number four.

His father then tells you how they usually spend their holidays. What does he say?

Mention any **two** things.

(m) **D'habitude on passe les vacances dans un pays chaud. On adore passer toute la journée sur la plage à bronzer, et on aime bien nager dans la mer.**

(30 seconds)

(t) Question number five.

He then talks about the jobs he and his wife do. What does he say?

Complete the boxes.

(m) **Ma femme et moi, nous travaillons à plein temps et nous n'avons pas beaucoup de temps pour nous relaxer. Moi, je travaille dans une boulangerie et je dois me lever tôt le matin. Ma femme est infirmière et de temps en temps elle doit travailler jusqu'à dix heures du soir.**

(30 seconds)

(t) Question number six.

Antoine tells you about their holiday plans for the following year. What does he say?

Mention any **two** things.

(m) **L'année prochaine on a l'intention d'aller en Australie pour rendre visite à mon oncle et ma tante. C'est le vingt-cinquième anniversaire de leur mariage. Mes grands-parents vont nous accompagner.**

(30 seconds)

(t) Question number seven.

He then makes some suggestions about what you could do later in the week. What does he say?

Mention any **two** things.

(m) **Tu sais, il y a un petit lac à côté du camping où on peut faire de la planche à voile. Ou si tu veux, le matin, on peut faire une promenade, et l'après-midi, on peut louer des vélos.**

(30 seconds)

(t) Question number eight.

Antoine tells you about the jobs he and his sister have to do. What does he say?

Complete the boxes.

(m) **A la maison, c'est moi qui sors la poubelle et c'est ma soeur Mireille qui met la table. Mais ici au camping, je fais la vaisselle et Mireille achète le pain le matin.**

(30 seconds)

(t) Question number nine.

You talk to his older sister Mireille. She hates camping. Why?

Mention any **two** things.

(f) **Moi, je déteste faire du camping. Il n'y a pas grand'chose à faire pour les filles de mon âge. Mon petit copain n'est pas ici. Il est resté à la maison.**

(30 seconds)

[Turn over for Questions 10 and 11 on *Page four*

(t) Question number ten.

She tells you how she intends to spend the rest of the holidays. What does she say?

Mention **two** things.

(f) **Je vais rester au lit jusqu'à midi et je vais passer le reste de la journée à lire mon livre.**

(30 seconds)

(t) Question number eleven.

Antoine's mother invites you to stay for dinner. What will they be having to eat? What does she ask you to do first?

(i) **Si tu veux, tu peux dîner chez nous ce soir. On va manger le poisson que mon mari a attrapé cet après-midi. Mais d'abord, il faut demander la permission à tes parents.**

(30 seconds)

(t) End of test.

Now look over your answers.

[END OF TRANSCRIPT]

FOR OFFICIAL USE

G

Total Mark

1000/406

NATIONAL QUALIFICATIONS 2006

TUESDAY, 9 MAY 1.45 PM – 2.10 PM (APPROX)

FRENCH STANDARD GRADE
General Level
Listening

Fill in these boxes and read what is printed below.

Full name of centre

Town

Forename(s)

Surname

Date of birth
Day Month Year

Scottish candidate number

Number of seat

When you are told to do so, open your paper.

You will hear a number of short items in French. You will hear each item three times, then you will have time to write your answer.

Write your answers, **in English**, in this book, in the appropriate spaces.

You may take notes as you are listening to the French, but only in this paper.

You may **not** use a French dictionary.

You are not allowed to leave the examination room until the end of the test.

Before leaving the examination room you must give this book to the invigilator. If you do not, you may lose all the marks for this paper.

SCOTTISH QUALIFICATIONS AUTHORITY

©

Marks

You are spending your holidays with your family on a campsite in France.

Tu passes les vacances avec ta famille dans un camping en France.

1. When you arrive, you meet a French boy, Antoine. What does he ask you?

   _____

   1

   *   *   *   *   *

2. He introduces you to his family. His mother tells you about the campsite. What does she say? Tick (✓) **three** boxes.

   3

The campsite is big.	
It's really quiet.	
There are lots of tents.	
There is a lot for the children to do.	
There is a swimming pool.	
There is a football pitch.	

   *   *   *   *   *

3. She tells you about their journey to the campsite. What does she say? Complete the sentences.

   2

   We live _____ from the campsite. Normally the journey

   takes four hours but we were delayed because _____

   _____ .

   *   *   *   *   *

           Page two

Marks

4. His father then tells you how they usually spend their holidays. What does he say? Mention any **two** things.

2

_____

_____

* * * * *

5. He then talks about the jobs he and his wife do. What does he say? Complete the boxes.

4

	Job	Disadvantage
Father		
Mother		

* * * * *

6. Antoine tells you about their holiday plans for the following year. What does he say? Mention any **two** things.

2

_____

_____

* * * * *

7. He then makes some suggestions about what you could do later in the week. What does he say? Mention any **two** things.

2

_____

_____

* * * * *

[Turn over for Questions 8 to 11 on *Page four*

Marks

8. Antoine tells you about the jobs he and his sister have to do. What does he say? Complete the boxes.

4

	At Home	At the Campsite
Antoine		
Mireille		

*   *   *   *   *

9. You talk to his older sister Mireille. She hates camping. Why? Mention any **two** things.

2

_____

_____

*   *   *   *   *

10. She tells you how she intends to spend the rest of the holidays. What does she say? Mention **two** things.

2

_____

_____

*   *   *   *   *

11. Antoine's mother invites you to stay for dinner.

   (*a*) What will they be having to eat?

1

_____

   (*b*) What does she ask you to do first?

1

_____

*   *   *   *   *

Total (26)

[END OF QUESTION PAPER]

[BLANK PAGE]

FOR OFFICIAL USE

G

Total

1000/402

NATIONAL
QUALIFICATIONS
2007

WEDNESDAY, 9 MAY
10.05 AM – 10.50 AM

**FRENCH
STANDARD GRADE**
General Level
Reading

Fill in these boxes and read what is printed below.

Full name of centre

Town

Forename(s)

Surname

Date of birth
Day Month Year

Scottish candidate number

Number of seat

When you are told to do so, open your paper and write your answers **in English** in the spaces provided.

You may use a French dictionary.

Before leaving the examination room you must give this book to the invigilator. If you do not, you may lose all the marks for this paper.

SCOTTISH
QUALIFICATIONS
AUTHORITY

Marks

1. You read this article in a French magazine.

Les Tâches Ménagères.

Quelquefois, les filles s'occupent des tâches telles que laver le linge, faire les courses, passer l'aspirateur et faire la cuisine. Pourtant, certaines filles préfèrent laver la voiture et faire du jardinage.

(*a*) Which jobs do girls sometimes do around the house? Mention any **two** things.

2

_____

_____

(*b*) Which jobs do some girls prefer to do? Mention any **one**.

1

_____

Marks

2. A boy has written to the magazine about a girl he met.

Je n'ai pas fait le premier pas!

J'ai un petit problème. J'ai fait la connaissance d'une fille superbe, quand j'étais en vacances au bord de la mer. On s'est bien amusé, mais je n'ai pas eu le courage de lui dire que je l'aime. Rentré chez moi, je pense tout le temps à elle. Que faire?

Martin, 14 ans

Complete the sentences.

3

Martin met the girl when he was _____ .

He didn't have the courage to tell her that _____ .

Now that he's back home he _____ .

[Turn over

Marks

3. You read about a group of Spanish pupils who visited a school in France. Here are the opinions of some of the French pupils about the visit.

Des Espagnols en Bourgogne

> Au début, nous, on parlait français et eux, ils parlaient espagnol. C'était assez difficile, mais on s'exprimait par gestes.

Noël

> On a fait des progrès. Maintenant je sais quelques mots en espagnol. Je me suis fait beaucoup de copines et on s'écrit souvent maintenant.

Emeline

> On était soixante jeunes. Le soir on faisait des jeux et on avait du temps libre quand on était seuls sans les adultes.

Gerald

Who said the following? Write the correct name beside each statement.

4

There were 60 young people.	
I can say a few words in Spanish.	
We used gestures.	
We write to each other often.	

Marks

4. You read a letter from a girl who is looking for some advice about her future career.

> Salut à tous! Moi je suis Francine et j'habite à Lyon. Après le collège je voudrais devenir pompier. Le problème c'est que ma famille essaie de me décourager . . . ils disent que pompier, gendarme et pilote d'avion sont des métiers pour garçons. Que faire?

(*a*) What would Francine like to do when she leaves school?

1

_____

(*b*) How has her family reacted to her choice?

1

_____

(*c*) Why?

1

_____

[Turn over

Marks

5. You find this article about the island of Sri Lanka.

> Le Sri Lanka est un pays sous-développé. Même s'il possède 700 à 800 usines textiles et plusieurs importantes installations pour les activités touristiques, le Sri Lanka est principalement un pays agricole, avec beaucoup de grandes plantations de thé et de riz.

Complete the sentences.

Sri Lanka has between 700 and 800 _____ .

It has huge plantations where _____

and _____ are grown.

3

6. The article goes on.

> Le tsunami de décembre 2004 a eu des conséquences très graves sur le développement du pays. Un grand nombre d'habitants sont pêcheurs. Ils ont perdu leurs bateaux et ils ne peuvent plus exercer leur travail.

The tsunami caused huge problems in Sri Lanka. Why? Mention any **two** things.

2

_____

_____

_____

Marks

7. You read a letter from a girl who talks about her class.

Dans ma classe (5ème) les garçons sont super cool avec nous et ça, c'est bien! On joue au foot avec eux et on s'amuse bien. Les garçons, de leur côté, acceptent de venir aux boums qu'on organise! Dans ma classe, on fait de nouveaux amis facilement . . . je suis pour l'amitié garçons-filles.

Maryse

Are the following statements True **(T)** or False **(F)**?

3

The boys and girls play football together.	
The boys don't like going to parties.	
Maryse thinks it's easy to make friends in her class.	

8. Another girl talks about the boys in her class.

Dans les cours de maths je n'apprends rien, et c'est la faute des garçons. Ils n'écoutent pas le prof, ils font des bêtises et ils se moquent des filles. C'est injuste car on ne fait pas de progrès. En plus, le prof est toujours de mauvaise humeur — et je déteste ça. Je suis contre les classes mixtes.

Natalie

(*a*) According to Natalie how do the boys behave in the maths class? Mention any **two** things.

2

_____

_____

(*b*) Why does this upset her so much? Mention **one** thing.

1

_____

[Turn over

Marks

9. You read an article written by the French tennis player, Amélie Mauresmo.

Amélie : Ce que j'aime

J'aimerais avoir un chien, mais ce n'est pas compatible avec mes voyages. Ce sera pour plus tard, quand je ne jouerai plus.

J'adore le chocolat. Tous les jours je mange un dessert au chocolat. Et au petit déjeuner, je bois . . . du chocolat, bien sûr!

Pendant mon temps libre, j'adore rouler à toute vitesse en voiture ou faire du ski nautique. Je trouve ça fantastique!

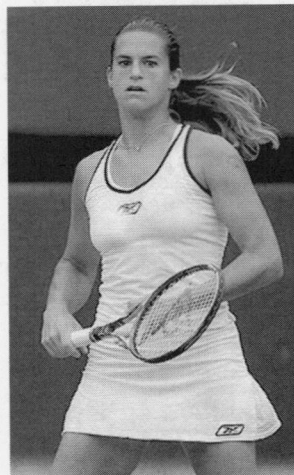

(a) Why does Amélie not have a dog?   **1**

_____

(b) What shows how much she loves chocolate? Mention **two** things.   **2**

_____

_____

(c) What does she like doing in her free time? Mention **two** things.   **2**

_____

_____

10. You read an article about how French people spend their free time.

Que font les Français pendant leur temps libre?

Avec la réduction du temps de travail, les Français ont plus de temps libre. Que font-ils avec ce temps?

La lecture est très populaire. Soixante-cinq pour cent des Français lisent régulièrement.

Les sorties sont aussi très importantes. Les Français aiment sortir au restaurant, au théâtre et au cinéma. Ils ont le plus grand nombre d'entrées au cinéma d'Europe.

Les sports les plus pratiqués sont la natation, le tennis et le football. Les hommes préfèrent les sports d'équipe et les femmes font plutôt les sports individuels.

Complete the sentences.

65% of French people _____ regularly.

French people _____ more than anybody else in Europe.

French men prefer _____ sports.

3

Total (32)

[*END OF QUESTION PAPER*]

[BLANK PAGE]

G

1000/407

NATIONAL
QUALIFICATIONS
2007

WEDNESDAY, 9 MAY
1.45 PM – 2.10 PM
(APPROX)

FRENCH
STANDARD GRADE
General Level
Listening Transcript

This paper must not be seen by any candidate.

The material overleaf is provided for use in an emergency only (eg the recording or equipment proving faulty) or where permission has been given in advance by SQA for the material to be read to candidates with additional support needs. The material must be read exactly as printed.

SCOTTISH
QUALIFICATIONS
AUTHORITY
©

Transcript—General Level

> **Instructions to reader(s):**
>
> For each item, read the English **once**, then read the French **three times**, with an interval of 5 seconds between the readings. On completion of the third reading, pause for the length of time indicated in brackets after each item, to allow the candidates to write their answers.
>
> Where special arrangements have been agreed in advance to allow the reading of the material, those sections marked **(f)** should be read by a female speaker and those marked **(m)** by a male: those sections marked **(t)** should be read by the teacher.

(t) You and your family are on holiday at a campsite in France.

(m) or (f) Tu passes les vacances avec ta famille dans un camping en France.

(t) Question number one.

When you arrive you go to reception. What are you asked for?

Complete the sentence.

(m) or (f)   Bienvenue messieurs-dames. Est-ce que vous avez vos passeports et une carte de crédit, s'il vous plaît?

(30 seconds)

(t) Question number two.

You are asked to pay a deposit in case of damages. How much do you have to pay?

Tick the correct box.

(m) or (f)   En cas de dégats il faut payer une caution de cent cinquante euros.

(30 seconds)

(t) Question number three.

You are told where your caravan is. Where is it exactly? What is nearby?

(m) or (f)   Votre caravane est située dans la troisième allée à gauche. C'est tout près du supermarché.

(30 seconds)

(t) Question number four.

When you have unpacked, you go to the swimming pool. You hear this announcement. What information are you given?

Complete the sentences.

(m) or (f)   La piscine est réservée aux adultes entre 18 heures et 19 heures. Toute personne de moins de seize ans doit sortir de l'eau dans vingt minutes.

(30 seconds)

(t) Question number five.

The next morning you take your little brother to the children's club. What activity is planned for that day?

) or (f)   Aujourd'hui pour tous les enfants il y aura un concours de boules sur la petite place.

(30 seconds)

(t) Question number six.

On Tuesday there is an outing to the beach. What are the children asked to do at 11 o'clock? What should they bring with them?

) or (f)   Mardi on va à la plage. Rendez-vous à onze heures à la réception. N'oubliez pas d'apporter quelque chose à manger.

(30 seconds)

(t) Question number seven.

You meet Jérôme, a boy from another part of France. What does he ask you?

Tick the **two** correct questions.

(m)   D'où viens-tu en Ecosse? Quand es-tu arrivé en France?

(30 seconds)

(t) Question number eight.

Jérôme tells you about himself. Where does he live? Why would he like to move?

Give any **one** reason.

(m)   J'habite dans un petit village mais je voudrais déménager car il n'y a rien à faire pour les jeunes. En plus, je ne vois pas souvent mes copains car ils habitent en ville.

(30 seconds)

(t) Question number nine.

He goes on to tell you about his holiday at the campsite.

Tick the **two** correct sentences.

(m)   Moi, je passe quinze jours ici avec ma tante parce que mes parents travaillent en juillet.

(30 seconds)

[Turn over for Questions 10 to 13 on *Page four*

(t) Question number ten.

Jérôme describes the jobs done by his mother and father. What does each of them do?

(m)   Mes parents travaillent tous les deux. Mon père est mécanicien et ma mère est vendeuse dans un grand magasin.

(30 seconds)

(t) Question number eleven.

What are Jérôme's plans for that day?

Mention **two** things.

(m) or (f)   Aujourd'hui, on va faire le tour de la région en car et on va visiter une ferme où on produit du fromage.

(30 seconds)

(t) Question number twelve.

Jérôme then suggests an activity which you could do together. What is he interested in? What does he suggest you could do?

(m)   Tu sais, je m'intéresse aux sports nautiques. Si tu veux, nous pourrions faire de la planche à voile demain. D'accord?

(30 seconds)

(t) Question number thirteen.

One of the entertainment team at the campsite speaks to you and Jérôme. What does she tell you?

Complete the sentences.

(f)   L'équipe d'animation invite les adolescents à un repas spécial ce soir à 20h30. Venez faire la connaissance d'autres jeunes dans le camping et découvrez les activités organisées pour vous.

(30 seconds)

(t) End of test.

Now look over your answers.

[END OF TRANSCRIPT]

FOR OFFICIAL USE

G

Total Mark

1000/406

NATIONAL QUALIFICATIONS 2007

WEDNESDAY, 9 MAY 1.45 PM – 2.10 PM (APPROX)

FRENCH STANDARD GRADE
General Level
Listening

Fill in these boxes and read what is printed below.

Full name of centre

Town

Forename(s)

Surname

Date of birth
Day Month Year   Scottish candidate number   Number of seat

When you are told to do so, open your paper.

You will hear a number of short items in French. You will hear each item three times, then you will have time to write your answer.

Write your answers, **in English**, in this book, in the appropriate spaces.

You may take notes as you are listening to the French, but only in this paper.

You may **not** use a French dictionary.

You are not allowed to leave the examination room until the end of the test.

Before leaving the examination room you must give this book to the invigilator. If you do not, you may lose all the marks for this paper.

SCOTTISH QUALIFICATIONS AUTHORITY

©

Marks

You and your family are on holiday at a campsite in France.

Tu passes les vacances avec ta famille dans un camping en France.

1. When you arrive you go to reception. What are you asked for? Complete the sentence.

   2

   Do you have your _____ and _____ ?

   *   *   *   *   *

2. You are asked to pay a deposit in case of damages. How much do you have to pay? Tick (✓) the correct box.

   1

   | 50 euros | | | 100 euros | | | 150 euros | |

   *   *   *   *   *

3. You are told where your caravan is.

   (*a*) Where is it exactly?   **1**

   _____

   (*b*) What is nearby?   **1**

   _____

   *   *   *   *   *

4. When you have unpacked, you go to the swimming pool. You hear this announcement. What information are you given? Complete the sentences.

   3

   The pool is _____ between 6 pm

   and 7 pm.

   Everyone _____ must get out of

   the pool in _____ .

   *   *   *   *   *

Marks

5. The next morning you take your little brother to the children's club. What activity is planned for that day?

1

_____

* * * * *

6. On Tuesday there is an outing to the beach.

(*a*) What are the children asked to do at 11 o'clock?

1

_____

(*b*) What should they bring with them?

1

_____

* * * * *

7. You meet Jérôme, a boy from another part of France. What does he ask you? Tick (✓) the **two** correct questions.

2

How did you travel from Scotland?	
Where in Scotland are you from?	
When did you arrive in France?	
How long are you spending in France?	

* * * * *

[Turn over

Page three

Marks

8. Jérôme tells you about himself.

   (*a*)   Where does he live?

           _____

1

   (*b*)   Why would he like to move? Give any **one** reason.

           _____

1

*   *   *   *   *

9. He goes on to tell you about his holiday at the campsite. Tick (✓) the **two** correct sentences.

2

Jérôme is spending one week on holiday there.	
Jérôme is spending two weeks on holiday there.	
He is on holiday with his grandmother.	
His parents travel a lot.	
His parents work in July.	

*   *   *   *   *

10. Jérôme describes the jobs done by his mother and father. What does each of them do?

2

Father: _____

Mother: _____

*   *   *   *   *

Marks
2

11. What are Jérôme's plans for that day? Mention **two** things.

_____

_____

*   *   *   *   *

12. Jérôme then suggests an activity which you could do together.

(*a*) What is he interested in?

    _____

1

(*b*) What does he suggest you could do?

    _____

1

*   *   *   *   *

13. One of the entertainment team at the campsite speaks to you and Jérôme. What does she tell you? Complete the sentences.

The entertainment team is inviting teenagers to a _____

this evening at 8.30 pm. Come along and meet _____

at the site and find out about _____.

3

*   *   *   *   *

Total (26)

[*END OF QUESTION PAPER*]

[BLANK PAGE]

[BLANK PAGE]

FOR OFFICIAL USE

G

1000/402

Total

NATIONAL QUALIFICATIONS 2008

TUESDAY, 13 MAY
10.05 AM – 10.50 AM

FRENCH
STANDARD GRADE
General Level
Reading

Fill in these boxes and read what is printed below.

Full name of centre

Town

Forename(s)

Surname

Date of birth
Day Month Year   Scottish candidate number   Number of seat

When you are told to do so, open your paper and write your answers **in English** in the spaces provided.

You may use a French dictionary.

Before leaving the examination room you must give this book to the invigilator. If you do not, you may lose all the marks for this paper.

SQA

PB 1000/402 6/36070

DO NOT
WRITE IN
THIS
MARGIN

Marks

1. You are reading a French magazine. This advert about a chain of restaurants attracts your attention.

RESTAURANTS «BONNE BOUFFE»

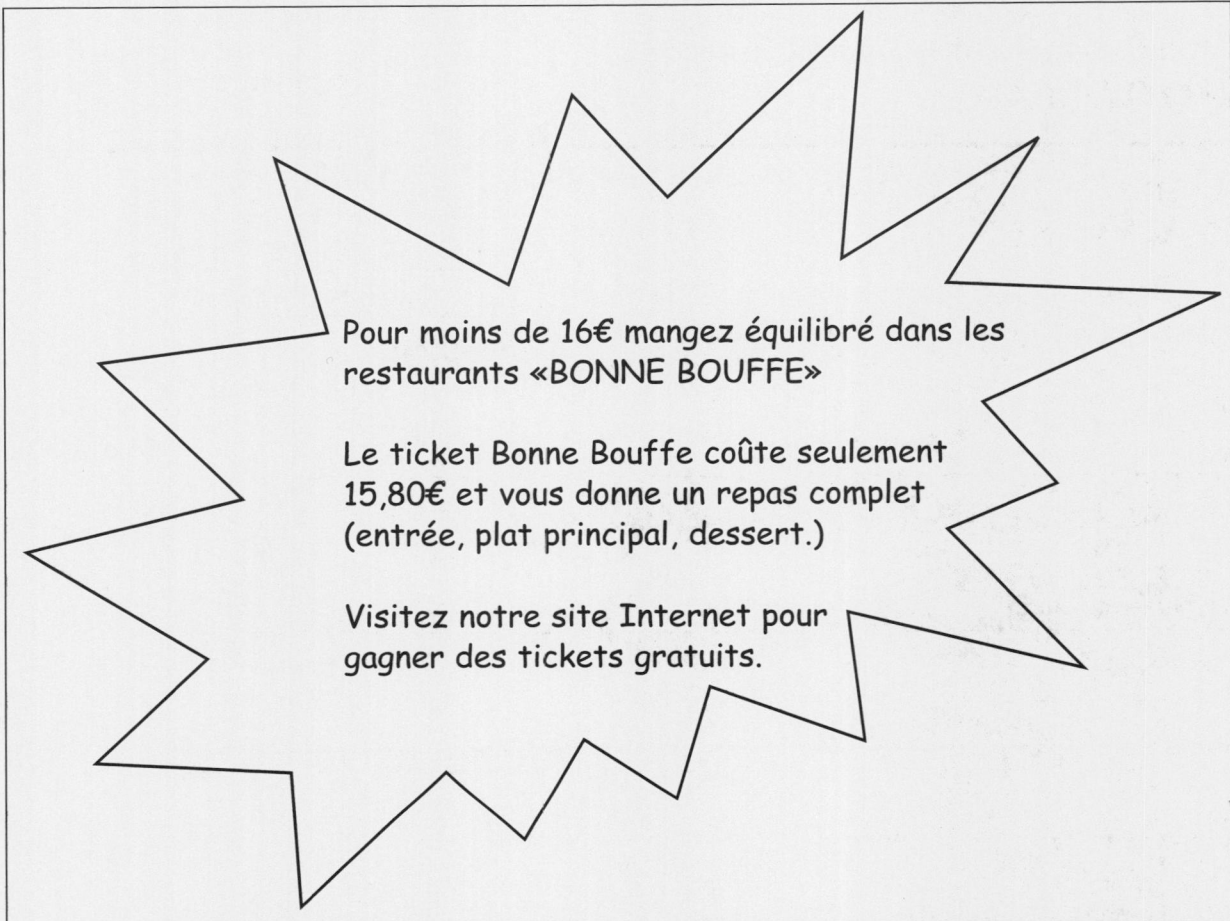

Pour moins de 16€ mangez équilibré dans les restaurants «BONNE BOUFFE»

Le ticket Bonne Bouffe coûte seulement 15,80€ et vous donne un repas complet (entrée, plat principal, dessert.)

Visitez notre site Internet pour gagner des tickets gratuits.

(*a*) What do you get for a 15,80€ ticket in these restaurants?   **1**

_____

(*b*) Why might you visit their website?   **1**

_____

Marks

2. You read about a survey on the eating habits of some people in France.

Bien manger, c'est un luxe?

Une étude récente indique que certaines personnes dans notre société se nourrissent mal et mettent leur santé en danger.

Ces personnes dépensent moins de cinq euros par jour sur la nourriture. Et aujourd'hui une barre chocolatée et un paquet de chips coûtent moins cher qu'un morceau de fromage ou de viande.

Pour ces personnes il y a beaucoup de risques de santé: l'obésité, les problèmes de coeur, les cancers etc.

La solution? Le gouvernement doit fournir à ces gens des produits frais qui sont meilleurs pour la santé.

et   ou   et   ?

Complete the sentences.

In France, some people eat badly and _____ in danger.

These people spend _____ per day on food.

The health risks are obesity, _____ and cancer.

The government should provide these people with _____

which are better for their health.

4

[Turn over

Marks

3. You read an article about helping airlines to trace lost luggage.

TRACEUR INTERNE

Placez à l'intérieur de votre bagage une étiquette portant votre nom, adresse et numéro de téléphone. Comme ça la compagnie aérienne peut retrouver le client quand l'étiquette extérieure a été arrachée.

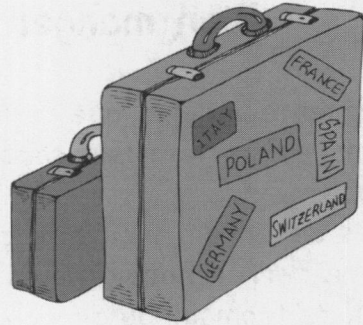

(*a*) What are you advised to put inside your luggage?　　1

_____

(*b*) When would this help the airline?　　1

_____

Marks

4. You read an advert about Toulouse airport.

---

www.toulouse.aeroport.fr

Nous vous souhaitons la bienvenue à bord de notre nouveau site Internet.

Il vous permet de choisir la meilleure offre, de réserver un vol à la dernière minute et de préparer un voyage d'affaires ou de loisirs . . .

On peut tout savoir sur l'aéroport Toulouse-Blagnac: les horaires, la location de voitures, et les tarifs des parkings par exemple.

Le monde aérien est à la portée de vos clics. Bon voyage!

(*a*) What services will this new Internet site provide? Mention any **two** things.

2

_____

_____

(*b*) What additional information can you find out about the airport? Mention any **two** things.

2

_____

_____

[Turn over

Page five

Marks

5. You read an article in which some French pupils give their opinions on school uniform.

Pour ou contre l'uniforme scolaire?

Je suis pour l'uniforme parce qu'il coûte moins cher que les vêtements à la mode, et les élèves travaillent mieux quand on porte l'uniforme.

Georges (Marseille)

Non à l'uniforme! J'ai horreur de porter une veste et une cravate en classe. Je veux choisir mes vêtements pour aller au collège.

Marcel (Bordeaux)

Moi, je suis absolument pour l'uniforme! Tout le monde s'habille de la même manière, donc il n'y a pas de distinction entre les élèves.

Adrienne (Paris)

Je dis "Non!" à l'uniforme au collège! Les vêtements qu'on porte font partie du caractère d'une personne. On doit être libre de s'exprimer comme on veut.

Estelle (Lyon)

Who says . . . ?

3

I want to choose my school clothes.	
Everyone dresses in the same way.	
A uniform costs less than fashionable clothes.	

Marks

6. Alain has written in to the magazine to complain about what he has to do at home.

Je m'occupe de tout à la maison

Pendant les grandes vacances je passe mes journées à la maison. En semaine, je dois surveiller ma petite soeur parce que mes parents sont tous les deux au travail.

Je dois aussi faire le ménage et préparer le repas du soir. Je n'ai pas un moment à moi. Que dois-je faire?

Alain, 16 ans

Tick (✔) **True** or **False** for each sentence.

4

	True	False
Alain has to look after his little sister at weekends.		
His parents are both out at work.		
Alain also has to do the gardening.		
He has to make the evening meal.		

[Turn over

Marks

7. Éric, the magazine's adviser, has written a reply to Alain.

Il faut aider à la maison, mais . . .

Je voudrais savoir combien d'heures par jour tu travailles à la maison.

Il est normal que les adolescents aident un peu à la maison, comme par exemple faire leur lit, ranger leur chambre ou faire la vaisselle.

Mais tes parents doivent comprendre que tu dois aussi avoir le temps de mener ta vie—pour faire du sport, pour écouter de la musique ou pour sortir avec tes amis.

La solution?   Tu dois discuter de cette question avec tes parents.

Éric

Complete the sentences.

5

Éric wants to know _____ Alain works at home.

Éric thinks young people should make their bed, _____

or _____ .

Alain should also have time for doing sport, _____

or _____ .

DO NOT WRITE IN THIS MARGIN

Marks

8. You read an article about the "Famille Nombreuse" discount card which is available to families with more than two children.

LA CARTE FAMILLE NOMBREUSE

La carte "Famille Nombreuse" existe déjà: les familles avec plus de deux enfants bénéficient d'une réduction de tarif quand elles prennent le train.

A partir du mois de juillet la carte donnera aussi droit à des baisses de prix dans certains magasins d'électroménager et dans les piscines municipales. En 2009 on va voir aussi des auto-écoles, des compagnies d'assurances et des vendeurs d'automobiles sur la liste. Le gouvernement espère ainsi qu'un nombre important de familles nombreuses va profiter de la carte.

(*a*) At the moment, what is the benefit of using the "Famille Nombreuse" card?

_____

1

(*b*) From July some places will offer price reductions. Mention any **one** place.

_____

1

(*c*) Who will join the scheme in 2009? Mention any **one** group.

_____

1

[Turn over

DO NOT
WRITE IN
THIS
MARGIN

Marks

9. Michelle Dumoulin writes about her job as a flight attendant.

Hôtesse de l'air

Je travaille comme hôtesse de l'air depuis sept ans.

Après le baccalauréat*, j'ai dû faire une épreuve de langue anglaise pour la compagnie aérienne. Pour faire ce métier il faut parler très bien anglais.

Bien sûr, pendant les vols, je distribue les repas, je sers les boissons et je m'occupe du confort des passagers.

Mais j'ai aussi un rôle très important dans l'avion. En cas d'incidents, je dois rassurer les passagers et les aider à sortir de l'avion.

---

*le baccalauréat = school leaving examination

(a) After the baccalauréat, what did Michelle have to do to get the job?　　**1**

_____

(b) What does Michelle do during flights? Mention any **two** things.　　**2**

_____

_____

(c) What does she have to do if there is an incident during a flight? Mention **two** things.　　**2**

_____

_____

Total (32)

[END OF QUESTION PAPER]

G

1000/407

NATIONAL
QUALIFICATIONS
2008

TUESDAY, 13 MAY
1.45 PM – 2.10 PM
(APPROX)

FRENCH
STANDARD GRADE
General Level
Listening Transcript

This paper must not be seen by any candidate.

The material overleaf is provided for use in an emergency only (eg the recording or equipment proving faulty) or where permission has been given in advance by SQA for the material to be read to candidates with additional support needs. The material must be read exactly as printed.

✕SQA
©

Transcript—General Level

> **Instructions to reader(s):**
>
> For each item, read the English **once**, then read the French **three times**, with an interval of 5 seconds between the readings. On completion of the third reading, pause for the length of time indicated in brackets after each item, to allow the candidates to write their answers.
>
> Where special arrangements have been agreed in advance to allow the reading of the material, those sections marked **(f)** should be read by a female speaker and those marked **(m)** by a male: those sections marked **(t)** should be read by the teacher.

(t)   You are spending a holiday with your family at a hotel in France.

(m) or (f)   **Tu passes des vacances en famille dans un hôtel en France.**

(t)   **Question number one.**

When you arrive the receptionist gives you some information. Where is your room? When do they start serving breakfast?

(m)   **Alors, votre chambre est au deuxième étage. Le petit déjeuner est servi dans le restaurant à partir de sept heures et demie.**

(30 seconds)

(t)   **Question number two.**

What else does he tell you?

Complete the sentences.

(m)   **L'ascenseur est à droite. Il y a aussi une piscine pour les clients de l'hôtel. C'est gratuit.**

(30 seconds)

(t)   **Question number three.**

The receptionist tells you there is a football match on Tuesday. How far away is the stadium?

(m)   **Il y a un match de foot mardi soir. Le stade est à quinze minutes en voiture.**

(30 seconds)

(t)   You meet Nicolas, a French boy who is also staying at the hotel with his family.

Question number four.

Where do Nicolas and his family live? Why do they come here for holidays?

(m)   **Nous habitons à la campagne. Alors, passer les vacances au bord de la mer, c'est super.**

(30 seconds)

(t) Question number five.

Nicolas asks you two questions. What does he ask?

Tick **two** boxes.

(m)   **C'est ta première visite dans cette région? Tu restes combien de temps ici?**

(*30 seconds*)

(t) Question number six.

Nicolas tells you what you can do there. What does he say?

Mention any **two** things.

(m)   **On peut bronzer et faire de la planche à voile à la plage. Et, si tu aimes les chevaux, il y a un centre d'équitation.**

(*30 seconds*)

(t) Question number seven.

Nicolas talks about his sister. What does he say?

Tick **three** boxes.

(m)   **Ma soeur est très contente d'être en vacances ici. Pendant les vacances de Pâques elle a travaillé dur pour ses examens. Elle veut aller à l'université au mois d'octobre. Mais pour le moment elle peut s'amuser.**

(*30 seconds*)

(t) Question number eight.

Nicolas talks about his parents. What does his father do? Mention any **one** thing.

Where does his mother work?

(m)   **Mon père est propriétaire d'un magasin. Il vend des appareils électriques—par exemple des frigos et des machines à laver. Ma mère travaille dans l'Office de Tourisme dans notre ville.**

(*30 seconds*)

(t) Question number nine.

Nicolas' mother arrives and speaks to you. Why does she like coming here on holiday?

Mention any **two** things.

(f)   **J'aime bien venir ici en vacances. Il y a beaucoup à faire pour les jeunes. Alors, je peux passer du temps avec mon mari parce que les enfants font toujours des activités avec leurs copains.**

(*30 seconds*)

[Turn over for Questions 10 to 12 on *Page four*

(t)   **Question number ten.**

Nicolas makes a suggestion for the afternoon. What could you do? Mention any **one** thing.

Where and when does he suggest you meet?

(m)   **Tu aimes le cyclisme? Alors, cet après-midi on peut louer des vélos et faire un tour de la ville. Rendez-vous devant l'hôtel après le déjeuner.**

(30 seconds)

(t)   In the evening you eat in the hotel restaurant. Your waitress is a girl called Monique.

Question number eleven.

Monique tells you about herself. What does she say?

Tick **True** or **False** for each sentence.

(f)   **Je suis née ici et mes parents habitent toujours dans cette ville. Je suis étudiante à l'université de Toulouse. Je rentre ici chez mes parents en été et je passe trois mois à travailler dans cet hôtel.**

(30 seconds)

(t)   **Question number twelve.**

Monique talks about her future. What does she say?

Complete the sentences.

(f)   **A l'université je fais des études d'informatique. L'année prochaine je vais faire un stage en Allemagne. Après mes études, j'espère développer de nouveaux programmes pour les ordinateurs.**

(30 seconds)

(t)   **End of test.**

Now look over your answers.

[END OF TRANSCRIPT]

FOR OFFICIAL USE

G

Total Mark

1000/406

NATIONAL QUALIFICATIONS 2008

TUESDAY, 13 MAY 1.45 PM – 2.10 PM (APPROX)

FRENCH STANDARD GRADE General Level Listening

Fill in these boxes and read what is printed below.

Full name of centre

Town

Forename(s)

Surname

Date of birth
Day Month Year

Scottish candidate number

Number of seat

When you are told to do so, open your paper.

You will hear a number of short items in French. You will hear each item three times, then you will have time to write your answer.

Write your answers, **in English**, in this book, in the appropriate spaces.

You may take notes as you are listening to the French, but only in this book.

You may **not** use a French dictionary.

You are not allowed to leave the examination room until the end of the test.

Before leaving the examination room you must give this book to the invigilator. If you do not, you may lose all the marks for this paper.

SQA

PB 1000/406 6/36070

Marks

You are spending a holiday with your family at a hotel in France.

Tu passes des vacances en famille dans un hôtel en France.

1. When you arrive the receptionist gives you some information.

    (*a*) Where is your room?   1

    2nd floor ✓

    (*b*) When do they start serving breakfast?   ②   1

    _7·30 am_ ✓

              *   *   *   *   *

2. What else does he tell you? Complete the sentences.   2

    The lift is _____ X _____ .

    For hotel customers the swimming pool is _outside_ X ____ .

              *   *   *   *   *

3. The receptionist tells you there is a football match on Tuesday. How far away
   is the stadium?   1

    15 minutes in a car ✓   ①

              *   *   *   *   *

You meet Nicolas, a French boy who is also staying at the hotel with his family.

4. (*a*) Where do Nicolas and his family live?   ✓   1

    un ~~germany~~ the country

    (*b*) Why do they come here for holidays?   ✓   ②   1

    because the beach is great

              *   *   *   *   *

Marks

5. Nicolas asks you two questions. What does he ask? Tick (✓) **two** boxes.

2

Is this your first visit to this area?	✓
Do you like this area?	
How long did your journey take?	
How long are you staying here?	✓

*   *   *   *   *

6. Nicolas tells you what you can do there. What does he say? Mention any **two** things.

2

you can tan on the beach

you can go to the sports centre

*   *   *   *   *

7. Nicolas talks about his sister. What does he say? Tick (✓) **three** boxes.

3

His sister is happy to be on holiday.	✓
At Easter she went on holiday.	
At Easter she worked hard for her exams.	✓
She wants to go to university in England.	
She wants to go to university in October.	✓
She wants to get a job for the summer.	

*   *   *   *   *

[Turn over

DO NO
WRITE
THIS
MARGI

Marks

8. Nicolas talks about his parents.

(*a*) What does his father do? Mention any **one** thing.   1

he works repairing eletrical equipment
like fridges

(*b*) Where does his mother work?   1

office for
an tourist information centre

* * * * *

9. Nicolas' mother arrives and speaks to you.

Why does she like coming here on holiday? Mention any **two** things.   2

theres lots of activities to do
to see her friend Marie

* * * * *

10. Nicolas makes a suggestion for the afternoon.

(*a*) What could you do? Mention any **one** thing.   1

go cycling to see around the town.

(*b*) Where and when does he suggest you meet?   1

outside the hotel

* * * * *

DO NOT
WRITE IN
THIS
MARGIN

Marks

In the evening you eat in the hotel restaurant. Your waitress is a girl called Monique.

11. Monique tells you about herself. What does she say? Tick (✓) **True** or **False** for each sentence.

3

	True	False
Monique's parents no longer live in the town.	✓	
She has a holiday job in Toulouse.		✓
Each summer she works in the hotel for three months.	✓	

②

*   *   *   *   *

12. Monique talks about her future. What does she say? Complete the sentences.

3

Monique is studying ___~~com~~ It_____ ✓ _____at university.

Next year she is going to work _____.

She hopes to get a job developing ___*computers*___ ✓ ___.

*   *   *   *   *

②

Total (26)

[END OF QUESTION PAPER]

[BLANK PAGE]

[BLANK PAGE]

[BLANK PAGE]

[BLANK PAGE]

Acknowledgements

Leckie and Leckie is grateful to the copyright holders, as credited, for permission to use their material:

The following companies have very generously given permission to reproduce their copyright material free of charge:
Richard Young for a photograph of JK Rowling © Richard Young (2004 General Paper p 5);
Parc du Futuroscope for an article (2006 Reading paper p 7).